Chadder's TREASURE HUNT THEATER
Leader Manual

Treasure Hunt Bible Adventure

Loveland, Colorado

Chadder's Treasure Hunt Theater Leader Manual
Copyright © 1999 Group Publishing, Inc.

All rights reserved. No part of this book may be reproduced in any manner whatsoever without prior written permission from the publisher, except where noted on handouts and in the case of brief quotations embodied in critical articles and reviews. For information, write Permissions, Group Publishing, Inc., Dept. PD, P.O. Box 481, Loveland, CO 80539.

Credits
Treasure Hunt Bible Adventure Coordinator: Jody Brolsma
Author: Jan Kershner
Chief Creative Officer: Joani Schultz
Copy Editor: Pamela Shoup
Art Director: Kari K. Monson
Cover Art Director: Lisa Chandler
Cover Designers: Becky Hawley and Jerry Krutar
Computer Graphic Artist: Joyce Douglas
Cover Photographer: Craig DeMartino
Illustrators: Amy Bryant and Drew Rose
Rain Forest Art: Pat Allen
Rain Forest Art Photographer: Linda Bohm
Production Manager: Peggy Naylor

Unless otherwise noted, Scripture taken from the HOLY BIBLE, NEW INTERNATIONAL VERSION®. Copyright © 1973, 1978, 1984 by International Bible Society. Used by permission of Zondervan Publishing House. All rights reserved.

ISBN 0-7644-9915-7
Printed in the United States of America.
10 9 8 7 6 5 4 3 2 1   00 99

Welcome to
Treasure Hunt Bible Adventure! 5

Your Contribution to
Treasure Hunt Bible Adventure 6

The Overview 8

Gearing Up for the Adventure! 10

DAY 1 (The Bible shows us the way to trust.) 13

DAY 2 (The Bible shows us the way to love.) 19

DAY 3 (The Bible shows us the way to pray.) 23

DAY 4 (The Bible shows us the way to Jesus.) 28

DAY 5 (The Bible shows us the way to live.) 34

X marks the spot...for VBS excitement! Grab your compass, dust off your binoculars, and be sure your flashlight has batteries. You're hot on the trail to Treasure Hunt Bible Adventure, where kids discover Jesus—the greatest treasure of all! Your young adventurers will explore how the Bible maps the way to amazing riches, showing us the way to trust, love, pray, and live.

Kids begin each day's treasure hunt by doing fun motions to new as well as familiar Bible songs during Treasure Hunt Sing & Play. Then they'll join with their Clue Crews to dig into Bible Exploration, create a wealth of treasures in Craft Cave, experience "vine" dining at Treasure Treats, monkey around at Jungle Gym Games, and, of course, view *Chadder's Treasure Hunt Adventure* video.

Chadder's Treasure Hunt Theater is just one of seven Discovery Sites kids will explore each day at Treasure Hunt Bible Adventure. At each Discovery Site, kids will experience the daily Bible Point in a new way. During Chadder's Treasure Hunt Theater, kids will view daily video adventures featuring Chadder, a mischievous chipmunk who learns what it means to discover the Bible's treasures.

Leading Chadder's Treasure Hunt Theater is easy and fun!

You'll enjoy your role and be most successful as a Treasure Hunt Theater Leader if you

- know how to operate TV and VCR equipment,
- understand that video can be an effective learning tool for today's kids,
- enjoy facilitating group discussions and have an interest in Bible study skills,
- ask questions to help kids connect the Bible Point they've learned in the *Chadder's Treasure Hunt Adventure* video to their everyday lives, and
- model God's love in everything you say and do.

Your Contribution

Your Contribution to TREASURE HUNT BIBLE ADVENTURE

Here's what's expected of you before, during, and after Group's Treasure Hunt Bible Adventure:

Before TREASURE HUNT BIBLE ADVENTURE

A CLUE FOR YOU!

It may be helpful to meet with the Treasure Hunt Director and go over the supply list. Let the director know what supplies you have or can collect on your own and what supplies you'll need to purchase or collect from church members. Open communication makes your job even easier!

♣ Attend scheduled Treasure Hunt Bible Adventure leader training.
♣ Pray for the kids who will attend your church's Treasure Hunt Bible Adventure.
♣ Ask your Treasure Hunt Director (otherwise known as your church's VBS director) what you should wear to Treasure Hunt Bible Adventure. Discovery Site Leader T-shirts (available from Group Publishing or your local Christian bookstore) will help kids identify you—and help you identify other Discovery Site Leaders. If your Treasure Hunt Director doesn't order T-shirts, you may want to agree on another easily recognizable uniform, such as an explorer's vest, tan shorts, and hiking boots.
♣ Read this Chadder's Treasure Hunt Theater Leader Manual.
♣ Check all equipment to make sure it's working properly.
♣ Preview each day's video segment, and read over the corresponding discussion questions.
♣ Meet with the Treasure Time Finale Leader. Each day's Treasure Time Finale will be a fun, involving review of the day's Bible story. The Treasure Time Finale Leader will need all the Discovery Site Leaders available to make things go smoothly. Be prepared to assist with distributing, displaying, or collecting props as needed.

Field Test Findings

Consider supplying your preschooler group with its very own copy of the Chadder's Treasure Hunt Adventure video. That way you can avoid the time and energy needed to transport all those excited little ones from place to place. We found that with a group of approximately fifty preschoolers, two copies of the video work best.

During TREASURE HUNT BIBLE ADVENTURE

♣ Help the Treasure Hunt Sing & Play Leader demonstrate the motions to "I've Found Me a Treasure" on Day 1. You may have learned the motions in your leader training meeting.

♣ Welcome each new group of Clue Crews to Chadder's Treasure Hunt Theater. Each group consists of one-quarter of the total number of kids attending Treasure Hunt Bible Adventure. So you'll be leading four different groups each day, plus showing the video segment to the preschoolers. Preschoolers will discuss the video with their crew leaders during Preschool Bible Treasure Land.

♣ To help create a fun atmosphere and reinforce Bible learning, play the *Treasure Hunt Sing & Play* audiocassette or CD as kids enter and leave the room.

♣ Repeat the Bible Point often. It's important to say the Bible Point just as it's written. Repeating the Bible Point again and again will help children remember it and apply it to their lives. Kids will be listening for the Bible Point so they can respond by shouting "Eureka!" Each day's theater session suggests ways to include the Bible Point.

♣ Each day, Clue Crews will receive three clues for a Treasure Chest Quest. The Treasure Time Finale Leader is responsible for the Treasure Chest Quest and may ask you to distribute clues to the Clue Keepers in each Treasure Hunt Theater session.

♣ To avoid disrupting other Discovery Sites, keep kids in your room until you hear your Treasure Hunt Director's signal.

♣ Rewind the *Chadder's Treasure Hunt Adventure* video segment for each new group. Simply rewind the video until you see the title appear on screen, signaling the end of the previous day's segment. You'll have five minutes between groups to do this.

♣ Tell kids that they can purchase their own copies of *Chadder's Treasure Hunt Adventure* to watch at home after VBS. This is a great way to reinforce Bible learning and to help kids remember Treasure Hunt Bible Adventure all year long.

♣ Attend and participate in each day's Treasure Time Finale.

A Clue For You!

The Chadder's Treasure Hunt Adventure video also includes a bonus activity guide. Families will enjoy the activities that help children dig deeper into the Bible stories and themes from VBS.

After TREASURE HUNT BIBLE ADVENTURE

♣ Return equipment to its proper place. Return the *Chadder's Treasure Hunt Adventure* video to your Treasure Hunt Director.

♣ Remind kids of their mission of God's love all year by
- phoning neighborhood kids who participated in your Treasure Hunt Bible Adventure program,
- sending Treasure Hunt Bible Adventure follow-up postcards, and
- showing portions of *Chadder's Treasure Hunt Adventure* in your church's Sunday school or midweek programs.

▼▼ TREASURE HUNT BIBLE ADVENTURE OVERVIEW ▼

Here's what everyone else is doing! At Treasure Hunt Bible Adventure, the daily Bible Point is carefully integrated into each Discovery Site activity to reinforce Bible learning. Chadder's Treasure Hunt Theater activities are an important part of kids' overall learning experience.

	BIBLE POINT	BIBLE STORY	BIBLE VERSE	TREASURE HUNT SING & PLAY	CRAFT CAVE	JUNGLE GYM GAMES
DAY 1	The Bible shows us the way to trust.	Peter walks to Jesus on the Sea of Galilee (Matthew 14:22-33).	"Do not let your hearts be troubled. Trust in God" (John 14:1a).	• He's Got the Whole World in His Hands • The B-I-B-L-E • Where Do I Go? • I've Found Me a Treasure (chorus and verse 1)	**Craft** Jungle Gel **Application** Kids need to trust the Craft Cave Leader that Jungle Gel really works. In the same way, we need to trust God when things in life seem impossible.	**Games** • Swamp Squish • Peter's Windy Walk • The River Bend • Treasure Tag • Pass-Along Peter **Application** The Bible teaches us that God is powerful and that we can trust him.
DAY 2	The Bible shows us the way to love.	Jesus washes the disciples' feet (John 13:1-17).	"A new command I give you: Love one another" (John 13:34a).	• Put a Little Love in Your Heart • I've Found Me a Treasure (add verse 2) • Jesus Loves Me	**Craft** Operation Kid-to-Kid Magnetic Bible Bookmarks **Application** Just as the magnet links the two children on the bookmark together, the Bible connects us with others around the world.	**Games** • Monkeys Love Bananas • Footrace • Gold Coin Keep-Away • Firefly Fling • Mosquito Net **Application** As the Bible shows us how to love, we can love others.
DAY 3	The Bible shows us the way to pray.	Jesus prays for his disciples and all believers, and then he is arrested (John 17:1–18:11).	"I pray also for those who will believe in me through their message, that all of them may be one" (John 17:20a-21b).	• Let Us Pray • Hey Now • I've Found Me a Treasure (add verse 3)	**Craft** Surprise Treasure Chests **Application** When kids open the treasure chest, they'll be surprised at the "riches" inside. When we open our hearts to God in prayer, we'll be surprised by his loving response.	**Games** • Savor the Flavor • Centipede Scurry • Message Mime • It's a Jungle! • Flowers of Blessing **Application** It's easy to talk to God.
DAY 4	The Bible shows us the way to Jesus.	Jesus is crucified, rises again, and appears to Mary Magdalene (John 19:1–20:18).	"For God so loved the world that he gave his one and only Son, that whoever believes in him shall not perish but have eternal life" (John 3:16).	• He's Alive • Make Your Home in My Heart • Good News • Oh, How I Love Jesus • I've Found Me a Treasure (add verse 4)	**Craft** Good News Treasure Pouches **Application** The colorful beads on the Treasure Pouch will remind kids of the good news that Jesus died for our sins and rose again!	**Games** • Roll Away the Stone • Butterfly Breakout • Manic Monarchs • Jungle-Bird Jiggle • He Has Risen! **Application** Our lives can be changed because Jesus rose from the dead.
DAY 5	The Bible shows us the way to live.	Paul stands firm in his faith, even in a shipwreck (Acts 27:1-44).	"If you love me, you will obey what I command" (John 14:15).	• The B-I-B-L-E • Got a Reason for Livin' Again • I've Found Me a Treasure (entire song)	**Craft** Rain Forest Creatures **Application** Kids add color and "life" to Rain Forest Creatures just as God's Word adds color and meaning to our lives.	**Games** • Man-Overboard Tag • Out to Sea • Snake Swap • Crash Course • Cargo Toss **Application** Even when life seems scary or difficult, we can have confidence that God is in control.

This chart maps out the entire program at a glance. Refer to the chart to see how your Discovery Site activities supplement other activities to help kids discover Jesus—the greatest treasure of all.

TREASURE TREATS	CHADDER'S TREASURE HUNT THEATER	BIBLE EXPLORATION	TREASURE TIME FINALE
Snack Peter's Adventure Cakes **Application** Peter's adventure began when he trusted Jesus. Jesus wants us to trust him, too.	**Video Segment** Chadder and his friends begin searching for a hidden treasure. They stumble onto the deck of the SS Hope, where Wally the parrot warns them to watch out for Riverboat Bob. Chadder's afraid, so Ryan, the first mate, tells him to trust God. The kids go to Whistle Cave, followed by Ned and Pete, two scraggly sailors who want the treasure for themselves. The kids find the treasure map, moments before they're trapped by a cave-in! **Application** • Where do you turn when you're afraid? • How does the Bible help you trust in God? • Mark your Student Book at a Trust Verse.	**Peter Walks on Water** • Experience being in a ship during a storm. • Try walking on "water." • Discuss how Peter learned to trust Jesus.	• Watch how a pin can go into a balloon, without popping the balloon! • Use balloons to review the story of Peter walking on the water. • Receive gem treasures as reminders that we are precious to God.
Snack Love Chests **Application** Jesus showed love for his disciples when he washed their feet. Today's snack shows that love is a great treasure.	**Video Segment** Chadder sits in an old mine car, and the car takes off, racing through the cave. Near the cave exit stands Riverboat Bob. He hits the hand brake and Chadder goes flying, right into the boxes Ryan has been stacking on deck. Chadder thinks Ryan will be mad, but Ryan says he follows Jesus' example of showing love. Chadder leaves to look for his friends, but runs into Riverboat Bob instead! **Application** • Role play how you think Ryan will react to the mess Chadder made. • How can the Bible help you when it's hard to love someone? • How can the Love Verse you highlighted help you love this week?	**Jesus Washes the Disciples' Feet** • Go on a barefoot hunt to find the Upper Room. • Have their feet washed by their Clue Crew Leader. • Help wash their Clue Crew Leader's feet. • Help one another put their shoes back on.	• See how someone shows unexpected love to the Treasure Time Finale Leader. • Receive heart locks and keys as treasures to remind them that loving actions open people's hearts.
Snack Prayer Treasure Mix **Application** Jesus' prayer teaches us to pray. The items in the Prayer Treasure Mix remind kids to pray about specific things.	**Video Segment** Chadder awakes in the mine and finds Hayley and Tim. They find a clue and decide to ask Ryan for help. The kids find Ryan in prayer, and Ryan shows them the Bible story of Jesus praying. Chadder wanders off, and Colonel Mike sees him and mistakes him for a scoundrel. Colonel Mike tells Chadder to walk the plank. **Application** • Pray in your crew for the child who'll receive your Spanish Bible. • Is there ever a time when you shouldn't pray? Explain. • How can you pray as Jesus taught?	**Jesus Prays** • Learn ways to pray for themselves. • Practice praying for various groups of people. • Create a mural with their hand prints to represent Jesus' prayer for all believers.	• Watch a skit about what it might be like for God to listen to our prayers. • Receive magnifying glass treasures as reminders that prayer brings us closer to God.
Snack Empty Tombs **Application** On the third day, Jesus' tomb stood empty. These scrumptious snacks are empty, too.	**Video Segment** Ryan explains that Chadder's a friend, and Colonel Mike points the kids toward the monkey tree. Chadder loses the map, but Ryan assures him that Jesus is the real treasure. The wind blows the map back again, and the hunt continues. The kids find the treasure chest, and Chadder finds the key to the chest hidden in the old tree. Just as they open the chest, Ned and Pete step up to steal the treasure. **Application** • How do you get to heaven? • How can knowing the treasure of Jesus change your life? • Why is it important to know about the treasure of Jesus?	**Mary Magdalene at the Empty Tomb** • Experience the sadness of the crucifixion. • Hear Mary tell how she searched for her lost treasure—Jesus—at the empty tomb. • Hear "Jesus" call their names; then draw crosses on their mural hand prints to thank God for Jesus.	• Pray; then give their sins to "Jesus" and watch as he makes the sins disappear. • Receive personal messages from their Clue Crew Leaders that Jesus loves them. • Receive three gold coin treasures as reminders that Jesus is the most valuable treasure we have.
Snack Sailboat Sandwiches **Application** When Paul faced a shipwreck, his trust in God helped him. We can live an adventurous life when we believe in God.	**Video Segment** Ned and Pete plan to take the treasure, but Riverboat Bob steps in to help. Bob reveals that he's been watching over the kids all along. Colonel Mike wants to throw Ned and Pete to the alligators, but Ryan convinces him to show God's love. Hayley, Tim, and Chadder fantasize about what they'll do with the treasure, but decide to give the money to Colonel Mike to help him bring supplies and Bibles to people along the river. **Application** • How can the Bible help you make decisions this week? • What do you think about giving your Spanish Bible away? Why? • When are times you can use the Bible verses you marked this week?	**Paul Is Shipwrecked** • Be "handcuffed," and led inside a prisoner's ship. • Hear a fellow prisoner tell about Paul's experience in the ship. • Experience a shipwreck. • Discuss how Paul's life was in God's control.	• Use a "chirping parrot" to experience the importance of working together to tell others about Jesus. • Present their Spanish translations of the Gospel of John as a special offering. • Receive a compass as a reminder that the Bible gives us direction in life.

Gearing Up for the Adventure!

A CLUE FOR YOU!

The larger your TV, the better. A good rule of thumb is to have one inch of TV screen for each child. For example, a twenty-seven-inch TV would be adequate for about twenty-seven children. If your church doesn't have a large screen TV, you may want to consider borrowing one from a church member. If you'll have more than fifty kids in each session, you may want to consider adding a second TV. To connect the two TVs to a single VCR, refer to the diagram below.

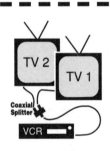

GEARING UP FOR THE ADVENTURE!

Discovery Site Preparation

🍀 Work with the Treasure Hunt Director to select a room for Chadder's Treasure Hunt Theater. If the Treasure Hunt Sing & Play Leader will be using Group's *Treasure Hunt Sing & Play Leader Training* video, you may want to consider meeting in the same room so you won't have to move equipment. For a true theater effect, choose a room that can be at least partially darkened.

🍀 Remove toys, books, or other items that might distract children.

🍀 Be sure to remove chairs from the room you'll be using. Preschoolers are much more fidgety when they're sitting in chairs, especially if their feet don't reach the floor. And elementary kids of different ages will have an easier time seeing the video if everyone sits on the floor.

🍀 Set up the TV and VCR. Practice connecting them, and then try playing, stopping, rewinding, and fast-forwarding the video.

🍀 Cue the *Chadder's Treasure Hunt Adventure* video to the appropriate day's segment.

🍀 Photocopy the sign and arrow from the inside covers of this manual. Make as many arrows as you need to guide kids to your room.

🍀 To create the feeling of a treasure hunt, transform your room into a tropical rain forest, complete with jungle shack! First, cut apart several cardboard refrigerator boxes and stand them in the corners of the room as the walls of your shack. Draw or cut out windows in each box.

Next, cut simple trailing vines from green butcher paper, and festoon them around the room, especially over the tops of the cardboard "walls." If you have a

dropped ceiling, hang vines from the dividers. If not, tape or trail the vines from corner to corner. (Green crepe paper streamers also make excellent vines!) You'll want to be able to make your room as dark as possible when viewing the Chadder video. If your room is air-conditioned, consider covering the windows with dark sheets or paper painted as deep green rain forest murals. If you need to be able to open the windows, use room darkening shades or drape dark cloth over as much of the windows as possible.

Perch colorful stuffed parrots, furry monkeys, funny frogs, and enormous rain forest bugs amid the greenery. You may even want to add a Chadder puppet to your rain forest! (Chadder puppets and large inflatable frogs are available from Group Publishing or your local Christian bookstore.) Then add some "jewels," and you're ready to go!

Field Test Findings

While you want your Chadder's Treasure Hunt Theater to look fun and exciting, make sure to leave room for the kids! Crews will want to spread out to read the Bible and pray, so decorate walls, corners, and ceiling, but leave plenty of space in the middle of the room. Also, keep distracting decorations (such as jewels and stuffed animals) to a minimum. This is the place kids really dig into the Bible, so time and attention are precious!

Discovery Site Supplies

- ○ a large color TV
- ○ a VCR
- ○ the *Chadder's Treasure Hunt Adventure* video*
- ○ Student Books* (one per child)
- ○ Treasure Hunt stickers* (one sheet per child)
- ○ Bible highlighters* (one per child)
- ○ a bamboo whistle* or another attention-getting device
- ○ a clock or a watch
- ○ the *Treasure Hunt Sing & Play* audiocassette* (optional)
- ○ a cassette player (optional)

* available from Group Publishing or your local Christian bookstore

A Clue For You!

Attention-getting signals let kids know when it's time to stop what they're doing and look at you. You can use the bamboo whistle (available from Group Publishing and your local Christian bookstore) or another noisemaker of your choice. The first time students come to your Discovery Site, introduce and rehearse your attention-getting signal. Once kids are familiar with the signal, regaining their attention will become automatic.

Discovery Site Safety Tips

♣ Set up your TV and VCR near an electrical outlet so children don't trip over the cords. If you must stretch cords across the room, tape them to the floor with electrical tape.

♣ If you choose to dim the lights while you're viewing the video, be sure everyone is seated first.

♣ Be sure to stop the VCR before attempting to rewind the video.

BIBLE POINT

✼ The Bible shows us the way to trust.

BIBLE BASIS

Matthew 14:22-33. Peter walks to Jesus on the Sea of Galilee.

When Jesus called, "Come, follow me," Peter didn't hesitate to abandon his fishing nets in obedience. As Jesus' disciple, Peter listened to Jesus' teachings, watched Jesus heal the sick, and witnessed Jesus' power over wind and waves. He believed that Jesus was the Son of God. Perhaps that's why, on the stormy Sea of Galilee, when Jesus said, "Come," Peter ventured from the safety of a boat and walked toward Jesus. The water may have been cold, the waves may have been high, and the wind may have stung his face, but Peter knew that the safest place to be was with Jesus. When Peter became afraid and began to sink, "Immediately, Jesus reached out his hand and caught him." In the arms of Jesus, Peter learned to trust. He later wrote, "Cast all your anxiety on him because he cares for you" (1 Peter 5:7).

The disciple Peter is the perfect picture of our humanity and weakness; he reminds us how desperately we need Jesus. Children feel that need just as keenly as adults. They're familiar with the fear that accompanies life's "storms"—when parents divorce, friends move away, pets die, and classmates tease. The children at your VBS need to know that, in the midst of those hard times, Jesus is calling them to "come." And when children step out in faith, Jesus will be there with open arms, ready to catch them. Today's activities will encourage children to cast all their worries upon a loving, compassionate, and mighty God.

Day 1

Theater Supplies

For today's adventure, you'll need
- the *Chadder's Treasure Hunt Adventure* video,
- a TV and VCR,
- Student Books,
- a Student Book from the Starter Kit,
- Treasure Hunt stickers (one sheet per child),
- Bible highlighters,
- pens or fine-tip markers,
- masking tape,
- chalkboard or large sheet of newsprint,
- the *Treasure Hunt Sing & Play* audiocassette (optional), and
- a cassette player (optional).

A Clue for You!

Check with your Treasure Hunt Director to see if he or she will be placing the Student Books in crew treasure bags ahead of time. If not, you can distribute the Student Books on Day 1 as each group comes to Chadder's Treasure Hunt Theater. Clue Crew Leaders will keep the Student Books in their crew treasure bags until the last day.

Chadder's Adventure Today

Chadder Chipmunk™ meets his friends Hayley and Tim to begin searching for a hidden treasure. Hayley has an old letter from her great grandfather that tells of a treasure map hidden in a cove. As the kids begin searching, they come upon the docked SS Hope. Ryan, the first mate, welcomes them, but says he can't help search because he's getting ready for an important voyage. But as he points them toward a nearby cave, Wally the parrot warns them to watch out for Riverboat Bob. Chadder's afraid of Riverboat Bob, so Ryan tells him to trust God, and gives him a Bible to help him trust. The kids go on to Whistle Cave, secretly followed by Ned and Pete, two scraggly sailors who want to take the treasure for themselves. In the cave, the kids are excited to find the treasure map. But moments later, a timber gives way and they're trapped inside the cave!

The Discovery Site

Before kids arrive, cue the *Chadder's Treasure Hunt Adventure* video to the segment for Day 1. You'll see the words, "Chadder's Treasure Hunt Adventure" and the logo.

Also before kids arrive, use masking tape to mark a large square on the floor. The square will need to be big enough so kids in each session can stand around it. Also, on a chalkboard, white board, or a large sheet of newsprint, draw a Reference Chart like the one on page 37. Displaying the chart will help kids and

Day 1

crew leaders keep on track during Bible study. Fill in the information for Day 1 on the chart, and hang the chart where everyone will be able to see it.

To help kids easily locate John 14:1, highlight the passage on page 26 of the Student Book found in the Starter Kit.

As kids arrive, welcome them to Chadder's Treasure Hunt Theater. When everyone is seated, say: **Hi, everybody! Welcome to Treasure Hunt Bible Adventure. Remember to give a loud "Eureka!" every time you hear the Bible Point this week. I want to hear how excited you are to be learning about the Bible!**

Each day when you visit Chadder's Treasure Hunt Theater, we'll watch part of our *Chadder's Treasure Hunt Adventure* video. You'll get to meet a crazy character named Chadder Chipmunk, who always seems to be getting into trouble. We'll see what kind of adventures Chadder Chipmunk gets into when he searches for lost treasure. You'll also discover what he learns about the Bible along the way.

All week at Chadder's Treasure Hunt Theater, we'll be hunting for the treasures in the Bible. And each day we'll mark our Bibles with clues. Today we're learning that 🎯 the Bible shows us the way to trust. (Eureka!) Let's watch our video and find out what Chadder learns about trust.

Play the Day 1 segment of the *Chadder's Treasure Hunt Adventure* video. Stop the tape when the action ends and the preview questions appear on the screen. Rewind the tape to the beginning of the Day 1 segment so you'll be ready for your next audience. Say: **Well! Chadder met lots of new friends today! And as usual, he got in lots of trouble!** Ask:

● **What kind of treasure do you think the kids might find?** (Jewels; money; gold.)

● **Why was Chadder afraid of Riverboat Bob?** (He's supposed to be mean; he might hurt Chadder; he didn't know what to expect.)

● **How do you think Chadder feels being trapped in the mine?** (Scared; sorry; lonely.)

Say: **Today we're learning that 🎯 the Bible shows us the way to trust. (Eureka!) But sometimes it's hard to trust—especially when you're scared or in trouble. Turn to a partner and tell about a time you were scared.**

Give children a few moments to share their thoughts and experiences. Then ask:

● **Who are some people you can trust to help you when you're scared?** (My mom; my dad; my grandmother.)

Let several kids answer, then say: **It's important to have people in our lives who we can trust. But it's even more important to learn that we can trust God. God will always be there for us and will never let us down.** Ask:

Field Test Findings

By leaving the Reference Chart up all week, kids will have a handy and quick way to check their Scripture references. By the second day, kids will already know to refer to the chart for the day's information.

BIBLE POINT

BIBLE POINT

A CLUE FOR YOU!

Clue Crew Leaders have a unique opportunity to get to know the kids in their Clue Crews. Encourage them to lead their Clue Crews in discussion, but don't be afraid to jump in and help if necessary.

Day 1

● **In our video, what did Ryan give Chadder to help him learn to trust God?** (A Bible.)

Say: **Ryan gave Chadder a little Bible. And that's exactly what I'm going to give each of you right now!**

Give each child a Student Book. (If your Treasure Hunt Director filled the crew treasure bags with Student Books, allow Clue Crew Leaders to distribute the books now.) Provide pens or fine-tip markers, and have kids write their names on the front of their Bibles. Then say: **These books actually contain the book of John from the Bible. Each day after our video, we'll look for treasures in these Bibles. And these Bibles are extra special! Look in the extra book at the front of your Bible.** Ask:

Field Test Findings

Having kids use the same version of the Bible made tabbing and highlighting extra easy. We highly recommend that you provide Student Books so kids can literally be on the same page!

● **What's different about the words you see there?** (They're in a different language; I can't read them; they're in Spanish.)

Say: **The words in this book are in Spanish. In fact, there's a whole other book of John attached to your Student Book. The Spanish Gospel of John is what you'll be giving away at the end of the week in Operation Kid-to-Kid™! Don't separate the Bibles yet—we'll do that on the last day of Treasure Hunt Bible Adventure. Right now, turn to page 2 in your Bible.** Ask:

● **Can anyone explain what that big number and those little numbers mean along the left side of the page?** (Let kids offer suggestions.)

Say: **The big number 1 at the beginning of the page means the chapter. This is Chapter 1 of the book of John. The little numbers are verse numbers. When we talk about verses in the Bible, we always say the book of the Bible first, then the chapter number, and then the verse number. So on this page, if I said to look up John 1:10, that would mean the book of John, the first chapter, verse number 10. Can everyone find that verse?**

Encourage crew leaders to help kids find the verse. Depending on how familiar your kids are with the Bible, you might want to practice with a few more examples.

Then say: **To help us learn to trust, let's look up a Trust Verse in our new Bibles. See if you can find John 14:1. It's on page 26 in your Bible, about halfway down the page.** Hold up the Student Book you've already highlighted, and show kids where the verse is on the page. Say: **After everyone finds the verse, have your Reader read the verse out loud.**

Since Readers have different skill levels, reading the verse aloud each day for the whole group will ensure that everyone hears it correctly.

When you see that everyone is finished reading, say: **I love this verse, so I'm going to read it out loud, too.** Read the verse aloud for the entire group.

Say: **In our video, Ryan showed Chadder that the Bible could help him trust God. I often turn to the Bible when I need to trust God.** Share a personal experience of a time you needed to trust God and how the Bible helped you.

Then say: **Today Chadder needed to trust God to help him with his fear of Riverboat Bob. And in our Bible story, Peter needed to trust**

Day 1

Jesus when he stepped out in faith to walk on the water. To help you when you need to trust God, we're going to mark our Bibles at our Trust Verse.

To do that, we'll put some clues in our Bibles to help us remember where today's Bible treasures are. You may not be used to marking in your Bibles at home, but we're going to really use these Student Books this week. To help you do that, each of you will get your very own **Bible highlighter.**

Have Clue Crew Leaders distribute the Bible highlighters. Say: **Go ahead and highlight John 14:1 in your Bible. Hold up your hand when you've finished.**

When kids have finished highlighting the Trust Verse, say: **Now we're going to put a Bible tab next to the verse we just highlighted. This will be your clue to help you remember where to turn in the Bible when you need to trust. The picture of the footprint can remind you how Peter stepped out in faith and trusted God. That way, when you need to trust God, you can turn right to this verse to help you.**

Have Crew Leaders help children find the footprint Bible tabs for Day 1 on their Treasure Hunt stickers. Each child will need one tab. Sound your bamboo whistle, and have everyone watch as you demonstrate how to apply the Bible tabs.

Say: **First, turn to page 26 where you highlighted the Trust Verse. Stick one end of the tab in the margin of the page, right next to the verse, but not covering up any of the words. Next, turn the page over and stick the other end of the tab in the margin on the back of the page. Now squeeze the tab together in half, and you have a tab marker for your Trust Verse!**

Field Test Findings

Don't be afraid to open up to your children. The more personal the experience you share with the kids, the more they'll be able to empathize and apply your experience to their own lives. Our Chadder's Treasure Hunt Theater Leader shared how reading the Bible helped her through a scary time when both of her children had heart surgery.

A Clue For You!

Pause after each step to allow kids to follow directions. Circulate among crews to offer help as needed. By the second day, you'll be amazed at how easy it is for kids to apply the tabs and stickers!

Day 1

A CLUE FOR YOU!

Since you may have new children in VBS each day, prepare a few extra Student Books to have on hand. After each day, highlight the passages and affix the appropriate tabs and stickers so newcomers the next day will have completed Bibles to take home at the end of the week.

🎯 BIBLE POINT

TREASURE CHEST QUEST

After kids have successfully applied their tabs, say: **Now you have a tab to show you a verse to read to help you trust God. Pretty cool, huh? You know, we've talked a lot about trust today. Let's do an experiment to see if we really know what it means.**

Have kids stand around the tape square on the floor. Tell kids not to let their toes cross the line. Ask:

● **How many of you think that the floor will hold you if you step inside this square?** (Most kids will answer in the affirmative.)

● **What makes you think the floor will hold you?** (That's what floors do; it always holds you; it's strong.)

● **What if I say that I don't trust this floor to hold you? What if I say you'll fall right through the floor?** (Kids will object to that notion.)

Say: **OK, let's try it. When I count to three, if you trust, step inside the square. One, two, three!** After kids step inside the square, say: **You were right—the floor *did* hold you! You trusted that it would because floors are meant to hold you, and it never let you down before. That's kind of how it is to trust God. He always holds us and never lets us down. All we have to do is trust and take a step in faith, just as Peter did.**

🎯 **The Bible shows us the way to trust.** (Eureka!) **Let's close by asking God to help us trust him this week.** Have kids join hands around the square. **Dear God, please help each person in this room learn to trust you more each day. And help us remember to turn to the Bible as we learn to trust you. In Jesus' name, amen.**

If the Treasure Time Finale Leader gave you **TREASURE CHEST QUEST** Clues, distribute them before kids leave. Have Clue Crew Leaders collect kids' Student Books. When you hear your Treasure Hunt Director's signal, dismiss kids to their next Discovery Site.

BIBLE POINT
❊ The Bible shows us the way to love.

BIBLE BASIS
John 13:1-17. Jesus washes the disciples' feet.

Jesus knew that his time on earth was coming to an end. His purpose would soon be accomplished, and he could return to heaven, to the side of the Father. Jesus' time with the disciples was coming to an end too. These followers, who gave up everything to follow Jesus and learn from him, must now carry his message to the world. What parting words would Jesus leave with them? How could he express his love for them and prepare them for the challenges ahead? Jesus' words were almost unnecessary, for his actions were unforgettable. The Son of God lowered himself to the position of a servant and washed his disciples' dusty feet. In this one simple act, Jesus demonstrated the depth of his love and modeled the servant's heart he desired in his followers.

It goes against human nature to put the needs of others ahead of our own. Our culture says to "look out for number one." We read magazines with titles such as Self and Moi. And we eat at restaurants where we can have it our way. Our world sends a self-centered and egocentric message to children, as well. That's why the children at your VBS can learn so much from Jesus' demonstration of love and humility. In today's activities, kids will experience the power of loving others through selfless acts. Children will discover that Jesus' actions are as unforgettable today as they were for the disciples nearly two thousand years ago.

Day 2

Theater Supplies

For today's adventure, you'll need
- the *Chadder's Treasure Hunt Adventure* video,
- a TV and VCR,
- Student Books,
- Bible highlighters,
- Treasure Hunt stickers,
- the *Treasure Hunt Sing & Play* audiocassette (optional), and
- a cassette player (optional).

Chadder's Adventure Today

Trapped inside the cave, the kids consult the treasure map they've found. They discover another tunnel in the cave, so they decide to explore. Ned and Pete continue sneaking behind. Later, the kids stop to look more closely at the map, which shows an odd-looking X with arcs at the top. Chadder plops down to rest in an old mine car, and Tim and Hayley head off in another direction, thinking Chadder is following. When Chadder accidentally hits a lever, the car takes off, gathering speed through the tunnel. Near the cave exit stands Riverboat Bob holding an ax handle. He hits the hand brake and Chadder goes flying, right into the boxes Ryan has been stacking on the boat deck. Chadder thinks Ryan will be mad, but Ryan says he follows Jesus' example of showing love. Chadder leaves to look for his friends but runs smack into Riverboat Bob instead! Chadder faints.

The Discovery Site

Before kids arrive, cue the *Chadder's Treasure Hunt Adventure* video to the segment for Day 2. You'll see the words "Chadder's Treasure Hunt Adventure" and the logo. The preview questions from the previous day's segment should help you find the right spot. Also before kids arrive, fill in the Day 2 information on your Reference Chart. Be sure to highlight John 13:34 so you can show kids where to find it in their Student Books.

As kids arrive, welcome them to Chadder's Treasure Hunt Theater. Say: **Greetings, Clue Crews! Welcome back to Chadder's Treasure Hunt Theater! Are you having fun at Treasure Hunt Bible Adventure? Turn to a friend and tell something you've enjoyed so far.**

After kids share, have a few children report their answers. Then say: **Today**

A CLUE FOR YOU!

Remember that whenever you say the Bible Point, kids will shout back "Eureka!" They'll enjoy surprising you if you forget!

Day 2

at Treasure Hunt Bible Adventure, we're learning that ✪ **the Bible shows us the way to love.** (Eureka!) **We'll learn how Jesus washed his disciples' feet as a way to teach them how to love.** Ask:

● **Who can remember where we left Chadder yesterday?** (He ran into Riverboat Bob; he fainted; he was looking for his friends.)

Say: **Let's see what happens to Chadder today.**

Play the Day 2 segment of the *Chadder's Treasure Hunt Adventure* video, but stop the tape just as Chadder lands in the boxes on the deck of the SS Hope. Turn on the lights if you had them dimmed.

Say: **Don't worry, we'll see the end of today's video. But first, let's act out what might happen between Chadder and Ryan. Ryan had just finished stacking all those boxes, and here comes Chadder knocking everything down.** Ask:

● **How do you think Ryan will react?** (He might be mad; he'll forgive Chadder.)

● **How would you feel if you were Ryan?** (I'd probably be mad; I'd make Chadder help clean up the mess he made.)

Say: **Turn to a partner. The person wearing the most blue will be Chadder, and the other person will be Ryan. Without any words, show how Ryan and Chadder might act if Ryan is angry. Maybe Ryan would shake his fist and Chadder would cry. You'll have thirty seconds to act out your scene.**

After thirty seconds, call time and say: **Now switch roles, and act out how Ryan and Chadder might behave if Ryan shows love instead of anger. Maybe they'll shake hands or Ryan will pat Chadder on the back. Ready? Go.**

After thirty seconds, call time again. Say: **Let's see what really happens.** Play the rest of the Day 2 segment of the video. Stop the tape after the preview questions. Later, while kids are involved in discussions, rewind the tape to the beginning of the Day 2 segment so you'll be ready for your next audience.

Say: **Well, Ryan could have been angry at Chadder, but he chose to show love instead.** Ask:

● **Where do you think Ryan learned how to show love?** (The Bible; his parents; church.)

● **Have you ever had trouble showing love to someone? Tell a partner what that was like.** (Answers will vary.)

Give kids a few moments to talk, then share a personal experience of your own.

Say: **The Bible is a great place to find out about love. Since Ryan said the Bible is his treasure map, I'll bet he learned how to show love by reading the Bible. Sounds like a good idea to me!** Have crew leaders distribute the Student Books, highlighters, and Treasure Hunt stickers.

Say: **The verse that we'll highlight today will show us the way to love. Turn to John 13:34 on page 25, and have your Reader read it**

✪ **BIBLE POINT**

Pair shares are a super way to get everyone involved. Shy or quiet kids are more willing to open up when sharing with a friend. You'll discover that this method of debriefing allows everyone to think, share, and participate!

Field Test Findings

Remember, sharing personal experiences can encourage kids to do the same. Our Chadder Treasure Hunt Theater Leader shared how she came home from VBS tired the day before and snapped at her son, who asked her to take him for a new bike tire. She explained that she would have done much better to have turned to the Love Verse as a reminder of how to show love.

Day 2

aloud for your crew. Hold up your prepared Bible, and show kids where the verse is on the page. Remind kids and crew leaders to refer to the chart on the wall.

When you see that most Readers have read the verse to their crews, sound your bamboo whistle to get kids' attention. Say: **I'll read the verse out loud for everyone, then you can each highlight the verse and put your heart tab next to it, just as we did yesterday for our Trust Verse.**

Circulate around the room to offer help and encouragement as needed. If there are new children in your group, give them each a Student Book you prepared in advance, and ask someone in their crew to explain what the tabs mean.

When kids have applied their tabs, say: ✹ **The Bible shows us the way to love.** (Eureka!) **This week, when you want to show love to someone, or you're having trouble showing love, turn to your heart tab. This verse, and the Bible story about Jesus, can really help!**

Before kids leave, distribute any **TREASURE CHEST QUEST** Clues you've been given. When you hear the Treasure Hunt Director's signal, dismiss kids to their next Discovery Site.

✹ BIBLE POINT

TREASURE CHEST QUEST

BIBLE POINT

✺ The Bible shows us the way to pray.

BIBLE BASIS

John 17:1–18:11. Jesus prays for his disciples and all believers, and then he is arrested.

We can only imagine the power and peace Jesus drew from his times in prayer. How he must have relished those all-too-brief moments—talking with the Father, pouring out his heart, praying for those he loved, and praising God. Perhaps that's why Jesus so often prayed privately, slipping away from the crowds to spend a few intimate hours with the heavenly Father. But this time was different. After the Passover meal, Jesus prayed, allowing his disciples to hear the burdens of his heart. And although the pain and suffering of the Cross were only hours away, Jesus prayed for his disciples and those they would lead. With his eyes turned toward heaven, Jesus spoke words of love and concern, words of finality and unity. In an intimate moment with the Father, Jesus spoke of those he loved and cared for…including you and me.

Although prayer is a key element in a child's relationship with God, praying can be difficult for children to understand or practice. Since they can't see God, children may feel confused about talking with God or disconnected when they try. That's why the kids at your VBS will appreciate today's activities. They'll learn that God really *does* hear our prayers, that we can use simple words when we pray, and that Jesus loved us so much that he prayed for us. Children will experience meaningful and creative prayers to help them discover the joy of spending time with God.

Day 3

Theater Supplies

For today's mission, you'll need
- *Chadder's Treasure Hunt Adventure* video,
- a TV and VCR,
- Student Books,
- Bible highlighters,
- Treasure Hunt stickers,
- ink pads,
- magnifying glasses (optional),
- audiocassette or CD of reflective music (optional),
- the *Treasure Hunt Sing & Play* audiocassette (optional), and
- a cassette player (optional).

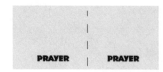

A CLUE FOR YOU!

If you can't find a CD or cassette of reflective music, use the song "Oh, How I Love Jesus" from the *Treasure Hunt Sing & Play* audiocassette or CD.

Chadder's Adventure Today

Chadder awakes in the mine and is surprised to see Hayley and Tim approaching around the corner. Chadder tells them of his encounter with Riverboat Bob, then they all sit down to discuss what to do next. Leaning against the wall are two pickaxes, crossed like an X. They realize the axes are the X marked on the map! They discover another clue under the axes that mentions a tree and a monkey, but the kids are stumped. They decide to go ask Ryan for help. Ned and Pete stumble and sneak along behind the kids. When Chadder, Tim, and Hayley arrive at the dock, they find Ryan in prayer. Ryan shows them the story in the Bible of how Jesus prayed, and explains that Jesus showed us the way to pray. Ryan says he doesn't know of a monkey tree in the area, but suggests asking Colonel Mike. Chadder wanders away from the group and pretends to be sailing the boat from the helm. Colonel Mike sees Chadder, mistakes him for a scoundrel, and tells him he'll have to walk the plank.

The Discovery Site

Before kids arrive, cue the *Chadder's Treasure Hunt Adventure* video to the segment for Day 3. You'll see the words "Chadder's Treasure Hunt" and the logo. The preview questions from the previous day's segment should help you find the right spot. Before kids arrive, fill in the Day 3 information on the Reference Chart. Highlight John 17:20 in your sample Student Book.

Day 3

As kids arrive, welcome them to Chadder's Treasure Hunt Theater. Say: **Welcome back to Chadder's Treasure Hunt Theater! It's been a great week so far at Treasure Hunt Bible Adventure! What's been your favorite part so far?** Allow a few children to respond, then continue: **Well, there's a lot more fun ahead. I wonder what Chadder will do today.**

Before you show today's segment of the video, review the week's story and Bible Points with the children. Encourage kids to help you finish these statements about the points. Say: **Before we watch the video, let's try to remember what treasures Chadder has learned about in the Bible so far. Let's see...the first day Chadder heard about Peter walking on water and learned that the Bible shows us the way to...(trust). Yesterday Chadder heard how Jesus washed his disciples' feet. Chadder learned that the Bible shows us the way to...(love). Today we're learning that ⊛ the Bible shows us the way to pray. (Eureka!) Since we're talking about prayer today, let's say a short prayer before we see what happens to Chadder.** Say a prayer similar to this one: **Dear God, thank you for this time together, and thank you for giving us the Bible. Help us to learn more about prayer today. In Jesus' name, amen.**

⊛ **BIBLE POINT**

Play the Day 3 segment of *Chadder's Treasure Hunt Adventure* video. Stop the tape after the preview questions. Later, while kids are involved in discussions, rewind the tape to the beginning of the Day 3 segment so you'll be ready for your next audience.

After the video, say: **Wow! It looks like Chadder really did it this time! This looks like a perfect time for him to start praying.** Ask:

● **When do you like to pray?** (At bedtime; before we eat dinner; when I'm scared.)

● **Is there ever a time when you can't pray? Why or why not?** (No, you can pray any time; God is always listening.)

● **What kinds of things do you pray about?** (I pray for my family; I ask God for help in school; I thank God for things.)

Say: **Praying is a wonderful way to stay in touch with God. He loves us and wants us to talk to him. Let's do that right now with a one-word prayer.** Have each crew sit in a circle. Continue: **Think of one thing you'd like to talk to God about today, and then think of one word that sums up your subject—kind of like a clue to what you're thinking. For example, if you'd like to ask God to help your Mom feel better, you could say "Mom" or "sickness." Or if you're thankful for VBS, you could say "thanks" or "VBS." You don't have to tell anyone what your clue means, but God will understand. I'll start the prayer, then you'll go around your circle and each say your one-word clue. Your crew leader will start. Then I'll end the prayer. Ready?**

Begin a prayer similar to this one: **Dear God, thank you for loving us and caring about us. Please hear each person as we tell you our**

Day 3

🔆 BIBLE POINT

A CLUE FOR YOU!

For extra fun, give each crew a magnifying glass. Kids can examine how their fingerprints are different from everyone else's.

- - - - - - - -

A CLUE FOR YOU!

Psst! We'll let you in on a secret! The Treasure Chest Quest treasure for today is a magnifying glass, symbolizing the way prayer brings us closer to God. If kids get to use a magnifying glass in Chadder's Treasure Hunt Theater, it will make a great connection when they receive one later!

- - - - - - - -

🔆 BIBLE POINT

thoughts right now. Pause as crew leaders and kids say their one-word prayers. When all is silent again, pray: **Thank you, God, for hearing each word spoken here today. And thank you for letting us talk to you. In Jesus' name, amen.**

Today we're learning that 🔆 **the Bible shows us the way to pray.** (Eureka!) **In today's Bible story, we see Jesus praying. The Prayer Verse we're going to highlight comes right from that story. Turn to John 17:20 in your Gospel of John—it's on page 30.** Have crew leaders distribute Student Books and highlighters to kids. Hold up a prepared Gospel of John and show kids where the verse is on the page. Remind kids to refer to the Reference Chart, and make sure to give prepared Bibles to any newcomers.

Have Readers in each crew read the verse aloud; then read it aloud yourself to the whole group. Ask:

● **Who do you think Jesus is talking about when he says, "I pray also for those who will believe in me through their message"?** (Everyone; us; all the people who would believe in him.)

Say: **Jesus was talking about everyone who would believe in Jesus because of what the disciples said and wrote in the Bible. And that means us—you, and me, and everyone else who believes in Jesus. I think that's amazing! Two thousand years ago, Jesus knew that you'd be born and what you'd be like, and he was already praying for you! Wow! This verse is really one to remember!**

Have kids highlight the verse and place the blank tab next to it. When kids have finished placing their tabs, say: **Each of us is different, but Jesus knows all about us and loves each one of us. Because we're each different, we're going to do something different with our tabs today. You'll notice that your tab is blank. That's because we're going to put our fingerprints on the tabs. Just as no two people's fingerprints are the same, no two people are the same. But we're all special to Jesus. Remember—we're so special to Jesus, that he prayed for us thousands of years ago!**

Distribute an ink pad to each crew. Say: **Use the ink pad to put your fingerprint on the sticker. Your pinkie will probably work best. We'll call these our prayer tabs.**

When kids have finished, say: **Today we're learning that 🔆 the Bible shows us the way to pray.** (Eureka!) **This week, remember to talk to God every day! Right now, let's close in prayer. Think of someone you'd like to pray for. Maybe it's someone in your family or one of your friends who needs to hear about Jesus. Or maybe it's the child who will receive your Spanish Bible. Remember—each person is special to Jesus. Then go around your circle, and crew members will each pray out loud for who they're thinking of. Your crew leader will start and end your prayer.**

Give crews several minutes to pray. If you brought reflective music, play it softly in the background.

Before kids leave, distribute any **TREASURE CHEST QUEST** Clues you've been given. When you hear the Director's signal, dismiss kids to their next Discovery Site.

TREASURE CHEST QUEST

BIBLE POINT

The Bible shows us the way to Jesus.

BIBLE BASIS

John 19:1–20:18. Jesus is crucified, rises again, and appears to Mary Magdalene.

Jesus' crucifixion was both a devastating and defining event for his followers. Although Peter, a close friend and disciple, denied knowing Jesus, Joseph of Arimathea and Nicodemus, who had been secret followers, came forward in their faith to bury Jesus. Even Mary Magdalene thought she'd lost her greatest treasure. Seeing the empty tomb, Mary probably assumed someone had stolen Jesus' body. Through her tears, she told the angels, "They have taken my Lord away, and I don't know where they have put him." Jesus, her treasure, was gone, and more than anything Mary wanted to find him. Mary didn't need to search for long. Jesus lovingly called her name, revealing himself and the miracle of his resurrection.

The greatest treasure children can find is Jesus. For in knowing Jesus, children will experience forgiveness, love, and eternal life. However, like Mary, the kids at your VBS may have trouble "seeing" Jesus. Mixed messages from the media, school, and non-Christian friends may confuse kids or mislead them. But just as Jesus called Mary by name, Jesus calls each of us by name, too. He knows the hearts and minds of the children at your VBS. Today's activities will help children discover that Jesus is the greatest treasure of all, and that he's right there, waiting for them with open arms.

Day 4

Theater Supplies

For today's mission, you'll need
- *Chadder's Treasure Hunt Adventure* video,
- a TV and VCR,
- Student Books,
- Bible highlighters,
- Treasure Hunt stickers,
- the *Treasure Hunt Sing & Play* audiocassette (optional),
- a cassette player (optional), and
- photocopies of the *Chadder's Treasure Hunt Adventure* video information letter (p. 33).

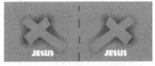

Chadder's Adventure Today

Ryan rescues Chadder from walking the plank, explaining to Colonel Mike that Chadder's a friend. Colonel Mike apologizes, stating that he thought Chadder might be an associate of those two lazy scalawags who used to sail with him. Of course, he's referring to Ned and Pete, who hear the remark from their hiding place nearby. The colonel takes the kids on a tour of his ship and explains the goodwill mission he's planning. The kids show Colonel Mike the clue about the monkey tree, and he points them in the right direction. On the way, Chadder accidentally loses the map, but Ryan assures him that they already have the real treasure—Jesus! As they walk along, the wind blows the map back in view, and the search continues. The kids cross a swinging bridge, and Ned and Pete follow, although Ned is awfully scared to cross. The kids find the monkey tree, and as Tim and Hayley search the area for clues, Chadder finds a key. The key contains another clue, and the kids finally find the treasure chest (with a little digging help from Chadder's paws!) They unlock the chest and find it full of jewels and money! Just then, Ned and Pete step up to steal the treasure.

A Clue for You!

Check with your Treasure Hunt Director to see if your church will have *Chadder's Treasure Hunt Adventure* videos available for families to purchase. If so, you'll need to add the information to the handout before you photocopy it.

The Discovery Site

Before kids arrive, cue the *Chadder's Treasure Hunt Adventure* video to the segment for Day 4. You'll see the words "Chadder's Treasure Hunt Adventure" and the logo. The preview questions from the previous day's segment should help you find the right spot. Also before kids arrive, fill in the Day 4 information on your

Day 4

A Clue for You!

Kids love watching Chadder all year long…and what a great way to extend kids' excitement about the treasure of Jesus! Often, families want to have new Christian videos, but may not easily find them. *Chadder's Treasure Hunt Adventure* video is an easy way for kids to share Bible truths with friends and family and to reinforce what they've learned at Treasure Hunt Bible Adventure for months to come.

A Clue for You!

In order for kids to get the most from this experience, don't correct any wrong answers to this question. Kids will understand your lesson as it unfolds!

A Clue for You!

Kids may not be familiar with the word "perish" from the Bible verse. Explain that "perish" means to die or be destroyed, especially in an eternal, spiritual sense.

Reference Chart. Use a highlighter to mark John 3:16 in your sample Student Book, as well as in the Spanish translation of the Gospel of John.

As kids arrive, welcome them to Chadder's Treasure Hunt Theater. Say: **Welcome back to Chadder's Treasure Hunt Theater! I'm really glad you're back for more of Chadder's adventures! What have you learned so far this week?** Review the week's Bible Points with the children.

Say: **What's your favorite part of *Chadder's Treasure Hunt Adventure* video so far?** Let kids respond. **Did you know that you can order your very own Chadder video?** Give each Materials Manager enough video information letters for his or her Clue Crew. Give kids a few moments to look over the letters, then have the crew leaders collect the letters and keep them in the crew treasure bags until after Treasure Time Finale.

Say: **Today we're learning that ⊛ the Bible shows us the way to Jesus.** (Eureka!) **We'll hear about Jesus' death and how he rose again. And we'll talk about why it's so important to believe in Jesus. Today we're going to do something different. Let's look up our Bible verse *before* we see the video. But we'll have to hurry, so there's time for everything.**

You may get a few moans and groans from the kids, but explain that they can see the video as soon as they finish their Bible study. You may get a few raised eyebrows from crew leaders as you appear to hurry through this important salvation message. But the impact comes later with a visual demonstration.

Say: **Before we get started, I have a question.** Ask:

• **How do you get to heaven?** Answers will vary.

Say: **OK—I was just wondering. Today we're learning that ⊛ the Bible shows us the way to Jesus.** (Eureka!) **Turn to John 3:16 in your Bible on page 5.** Hold up a prepared Gospel of John and show kids where the verse is on the page. Have the Readers read the verse aloud in their crews. Remind kids that they'll have to hurry to have time for the video. When kids have almost finished reading, say: **Since we're short on time today, I'll read the verse out loud quickly.** Read the verse aloud for the whole group.

Say: **Today's Bible story is about how Jesus died on the cross. In our video, the kids have been looking all week at a treasure map, where X marks the spot of the treasure. Our Bible tabs today have a cross on them that's slightly tilted to look like an X! That way, you'll remember that X marks the spot in your Bible for Jesus—the real treasure!**

Have kids highlight John 3:16 and place the cross tab next to the Jesus Verse. Encourage kids to hurry so you'll have time for the video.

As kids finish up, say: **Today's Jesus Verse is so important, I want you to highlight the verse in your Spanish Gospel of John, too. That way, the child who receives the Spanish Bible can go right to this important verse.** Hold up a prepared Gospel of John and show kids where the Spanish verse is. Have kids highlight John 3:16 in the Spanish section of their Bibles and place the other cross sticker from their sticker sheets there. Remind kids to hurry.

Day 4

When everyone is just about finished, say: **Is everyone finished? Now let's see what happens to Chadder.**

Before viewing the video, follow these instructions to bring kids to the realization that belief in Jesus is the only way to heaven. Pretend to be having trouble getting the video into the VCR. Instead of putting the cassette in horizontally, try to insert it vertically. Try it this way and that, in the front and the back, and talk out loud to yourself as you try. Make comments such as, "I'm sure I can do this," and "Maybe if I just try a little harder." Kids will begin to offer to help you, and will give you instructions how to succeed. Answer by saying: **No, this is something that I have to do myself—no one can do it for me.**

Pause now and then, and pretend to have an idea, saying: **I know! Maybe I can straighten up the room. I know if I just work a little harder I can do this!** Then pick up a few items before trying again. Or pause to ponder, saying: **I don't understand. I'm a good person. I go to church.**

Toward the end of your performance, say: **What I need is an instruction manual.** By this time, crew leaders and kids may suggest that you look in your Bible. Even if no one suggests it, stop and ask:

- **What is our instruction manual for life?** (The Bible.)
- **How many ways are there to put the video in the VCR?** (One.)
- **And how many ways are there to get into heaven?** (Just one!)
- **What is it?** (Believing in Jesus.)

Say: **Just as there's only one way to put the video into the VCR, there's only one way to get into heaven. And that's believing in Jesus. It's real simple, and it's real important. Because it's the only way.**

But just as I kept urging you to hurry, sometimes things in our lives urge us to hurry right past Jesus. We might get so caught up in school, or with friends or in sports, that we don't seem to have time to read our Bibles and remember that Jesus is the most important treasure there is. Sometimes, we might even get caught up in trying to earn our way to heaven. That's when we need to turn back to the Bible to remember that Jesus is the only way to get there. Hold up your Bible. **X marks the spot in your Bible for the most important treasure of all, Jesus! He's the only way into heaven!**

Got it? OK, *now* let's see what's going on with Chadder.

Play the Day 4 segment of *Chadder's Treasure Hunt Adventure* video.

After the video, say: ✪ **The Bible shows us the way to Jesus.** (Eureka!) **Because Jesus really did rise from the dead, all people who believe in Jesus can be forgiven and live with him in heaven. And that's why it's so important to share our faith—so others can believe, too!** ✪ **The Bible shows us the way to Jesus** (Eureka!), **and we can help others believe! Tomorrow we'll talk more about helping others believe. Until then, let's thank God for giving us Jesus.**

Have each Prayer Person lead a simple prayer for his or her crew, thanking

Field Test Findings

This is such a cool lesson! Kids were going crazy trying to explain the correct way to insert the video! As we watched, we could see the "light bulbs" going on in crew leaders' heads as they "caught on" to what was happening. Next, the kids "got it"! And it was a powerful, meaningful example for everyone.

A Clue For You!

As you pretend to try to force the video into the VCR, you may inadvertently hit some of the VCR control buttons. Don't be surprised if your volume or other control has changed!

Day 4

TREASURE CHEST QUEST

God for sending his Son to die for our sins. Give kids a few moments to pray, then close with a prayer similar to this one: **Dear God, thank you for sending your only Son to die for us and to rise again. Thank you for giving us the Bible to tell us about Jesus. In his name, amen.**

Before kids leave, distribute any **TREASURE CHEST QUEST** Clues you've been given. When you hear the Director's signal, dismiss kids to their next Discovery Site.

> If you sense that a child might like to know more about what it means to believe in Jesus, refer the child to your church's pastor. Or if you feel comfortable talking with the child yourself, give this simple explanation: **God loves us so much that he gave his Son, Jesus, to die on the cross for us. Jesus died and rose again so we could be forgiven for all the wrong things we do. If we ask him, Jesus will come into our lives. He'll always be with us and help us to make the right choices. If we believe in Jesus, someday we'll live with him forever in heaven.**
>
> You may want to lead the child in a simple prayer, inviting Jesus to be his or her Lord. Be sure to share the news of the child's spiritual development with his or her parent(s).

DEAR PARENT:

Each day this week, your child has enjoyed a video visit with Chadder Chipmunk™, our furry little Treasure Hunt Bible Adventure mascot.

Chadder is off on an exciting treasure hunt, along with friends Tim and Hayley. Along the way, they get help and advice from Colonel Mike and his first mate, Ryan, who shares his faith with the kids.

But they're not alone! Ned and Pete, two bumbling scalawags, want the treasure, too, and mysterious Riverboat Bob seems to be following Chadder in his search. But through it all, Chadder and his friends learn that the Bible is their real treasure map and that Jesus is the treasure!

CHADDER'S TREASURE HUNT ADVENTURE video teaches positive, practical ways for your child to meet challenges—and reinforces solid Bible values.

You can purchase a copy of **CHADDER'S TREASURE HUNT ADVENTURE** at your local Christian bookstore. While watching this video at home, your child will be reminded of this week's fun, Bible-learning experiences...and you'll enjoy watching it, too. Plus, each video includes a bonus family activity guide, bursting with great ideas for families to explore Bible truths and stories in captivating, memorable ways.

Thanks for encouraging your child to visit Treasure Hunt Bible Adventure. It's been a privilege to share this week with your child.

Sincerely,

Chadder's Treasure Hunt Theater Leader

P.S. To order **CHADDER'S TREASURE HUNT ADVENTURE** video, check with your church's VBS Director, visit your local Christian bookstore, or contact Group Publishing.

Permission to photocopy this letter from Treasure Hunt Bible Adventure: Chadder's Treasure Hunt Theater granted for local church use. Copyright © Group Publishing, Inc., P.O. Box 481, Loveland, CO 80539.

BIBLE POINT

✿ The Bible shows us the way to live.

BIBLE BASIS

Acts 27:1-44. Paul stands firm in his faith, even in a shipwreck.

After Paul came to believe in Jesus, he fervently shared the news of Jesus everywhere he went. In Jerusalem, Paul encountered a group of men who opposed his teachings. These men incited a riot, accusing Paul of teaching false doctrine and of defiling the Temple. In the confusion of the angry mob, Paul was arrested and thrown in prison. The following years included trials, death threats, confused centurions, secret transfers to other prisons, and finally a trip to Rome where Paul could plead his case before Caesar. As if Paul hadn't encountered enough trouble, his ship ran into a violent storm and was eventually shipwrecked! Throughout the ordeal, Paul's faith remained strong. He prayed with other prisoners, encouraged his captors to be courageous, and shared his faith in God with everyone on board. Even in the worst circumstances, Paul's life reflected the power of Christ's love.

Most of the children in your VBS won't encounter the kind of persecution that Paul faced. But they'll face tough decisions, peer pressure, false religions, and secular advice that will challenge their faith. That's why it's important for kids to use God's Word as their map for life, a tool to guide them through the storms and "shipwrecks" along the way. Use today's activities to show children the power in the Bible and to help them discover its usefulness in successfully navigating life's everyday trials.

Day 5

Theater Supplies

For today's mission, you'll need
- ○ *Chadder's Treasure Hunt Adventure* video,
- ○ a TV and VCR,
- ○ Student Books,
- ○ Bible highlighters,
- ○ Treasure Hunt stickers,
- ○ the *Treasure Hunt Sing & Play* audiocassette (optional), and
- ○ a cassette player (optional).

Chadder's Adventure Today

As Ned and Pete try to take the treasure the kids found, Riverboat Bob steps in to help. Riverboat Bob lifts Ned and Pete off their feet, and Chadder shakes with fear. But Riverboat Bob reveals to Chadder that he's been watching over the kids all along. Back at the ship, with Ned and Pete safely tied up, Colonel Mike wants to throw the villains to the alligators. But Ryan convinces him to show God's love. Colonel Mike agrees. Hayley, Tim, and Chadder fantasize about what they'll do with the treasure, but decide to give the money to Colonel Mike to help him bring supplies and Bibles to people along the river. Colonel Mike is upset when he sees Riverboat Bob, accusing him of deserting the ship years ago when he was navigator. Riverboat Bob explains that he had gone for help, and the ship was gone when he returned. He thought *he* had been deserted! Colonel Mike and Riverboat Bob, forgive each other, and agree to work together on the mission of love. The story ends with all hands on deck getting ready for the big voyage to help others.

The Discovery Site

Before kids arrive, cue the *Chadder's Treasure Hunt Adventure* video to the segment for Day 5. You'll see the words "Chadder's Treasure Hunt Adventure" and the logo. The preview questions from the previous day's segment should help you find the right spot. Also before kids arrive, fill in the Day 5 information on the Reference Chart. Highlight John 14:15 in your sample Student Book.

As kids arrive, welcome them to Chadder's Treasure Hunt Theater. Say: **Welcome to the last day at Chadder's Treasure Hunt Theater! I've really enjoyed seeing you each day!** Ask:

Day 5

● **Who can tell me what today's Bible Point is?** (Let kids shout out the point and response.)

Then say: **The Bible really is like a treasure map for our lives, because it gives us directions for how to live. When we turn to the Bible and see what God has to say, amazing things happen. What do you think might happen with Chadder today?** Let kids respond.

Then say: **Well, let's see if you're right.** Play the Day 5 segment of *Chadder's Treasure Hunt Adventure* video. Stop the tape when the closing credits roll. There are no preview questions for Day 5. Later, while kids are involved in discussions, rewind the tape to the beginning of the Day 5 segment so you'll be ready for your next audience.

Say: **Wow! What a great ending to *Chadder's Treasure Hunt Adventure*. I'm going to ask a few questions for you to discuss in your crews. We'll start with the Cheerleaders and move around the group to the right, so everyone can answer.** Ask:

● **What surprised you about today's video segment?** (I was surprised they gave the treasure away; that Ned and Pete got caught; at who Riverboat was.)

● **Would you have given the treasure away as Chadder and the kids did? Why or why not?** (Answers will vary.)

Say: **Our Bible story today shows us how Paul's faith helped him in a scary situation and how he was able to help others.** Ask:

● **In the video, how did Ryan's faith help others?** (He gave Ned and Pete another chance; he helped Chadder see how important the Bible is.)

● **How can your faith help others this week?** (I can tell someone about Jesus; I can pray; I can share my Bible.)

Say: **Our Bible tab today has an arrow on it, to remind us that ✪ the Bible shows us the way to live.** (Eureka!) **Just as the arrow on a compass tells you which way to go, the Bible is like our compass in life.**

Tell crews to turn to John 14:15 on page 26, and have their Readers read the verse. When Readers have finished, read the verse aloud for the group. Then have kids highlight the Live Verse and place the arrow tab next to it.

Say: **When you get home, you might want to mark your own Bible with some of the same verses we highlighted this week. You can even mark other verses you like! I hope you really use these Bible tabs at home, because the Bible is such a great treasure to turn to.** Ask:

● **If you were upset because someone you loved was sick, which Bible tab could you use?** (The footprint tab; the prayer tab; the arrow tab.)

● **How about if you're mad at someone?** (The heart tab; the prayer tab; the arrow tab.)

Say: **Just as Chadder and his friends gave their treasure away to help others, you have a treasure to give away too. Today's the day you get to share your faith and give away your Spanish Bible.** Ask:

● **How can the Bibles you're giving away help other children?**

A CLUE FOR YOU!

This is a great time to check with kids and see if they have Bibles at home.

✪ BIBLE POINT

Field Test Findings

During this time of assessment, you'll be amazed at how well the kids grasp how to use the Bible tabs. The kids in the field test really thought about how to use the Bible and how the tabs could direct them to appropriate verses. And after our last Treasure Time Finale, not one Student Book was left behind!

(They can teach them about Jesus; show them how to live; help them when they're scared.)

● **How can the Bible help you this coming week?** (It can help me pray; help me remember about Jesus; help me know what to do.)

Say: **Let's add a special sticker to the Bibles to let these children know that the Bible is a special gift of love from you.** Point to the Gift of Love sticker on the Treasure Hunt stickers sheet. **First, place this sticker inside the cover of the Spanish Bible.** Then, sign your name underneath the sticker. Now, the page reads "A gift of love from your friend" and your name. Allow a few moments for Clue Crews to work together and place the Gift of Love stickers in the appropriate places.

Say: ❂ **The Bible shows us the way to live.** (Eureka!) **This week, and the week after that, remember to use your Bible. It's your treasure map that leads to Jesus—the greatest treasure of all! Before you leave, let's have one last prayer together. But let's not shout "Eureka!" until after we say "amen."**

Pray a prayer similar to this one: **Dear God, thank you for the fun we've had this week and the things we've learned about you and the Bible. Help us remember that the Bible shows us the way to trust, to love, to pray, to find Jesus, and to live. Thank you, God, for loving us so much. In Jesus' name, amen. "Eureka!"**

❂ **BIBLE POINT**

DAILY REFERENCE CHART

Day	The Bible Shows Us the Way to...	Location of Bible Verse and Tab	Bible Tab Clue	The Bible Story
Day 1	Trust	John 14:1 (page 26)		Peter walks on water (Matthew 14:22-33)
Day 2	Love	John 13:34 (page 25)		Jesus washes his disciples' feet (John 13:1-17)
Day 3	Pray	John 17:20 (page 30)		Jesus prays (John 17:1–18:11)
Day 4	Jesus	John 3:16 (page 5)		Jesus' death and resurrection (John 19:1–20:18)
Day 5	Live	John 14:15 (page 26)		Paul's shipwreck (Acts 27:1-44)

TEACH YOUR PRESCHOOLERS AS JESUS TAUGHT WITH GROUP'S *HANDS-ON BIBLE CURRICULUM*™

Hands-On Bible Curriculum™ for preschoolers helps your preschoolers learn the way they learn best—by touching, exploring, and discovering. With active and authentic learning, preschoolers love learning about the Bible, and they really remember what they learn.

Because small children learn best through repetition, Preschoolers and Pre-K & K will learn one important point per lesson, and Toddlers & 2s will learn one point each month with **Hands-On Bible Curriculum**. These important lessons will stick with them and comfort them during their daily lives. Your children will learn God is our friend, who Jesus is, and we can always trust Jesus.

The **Learning Lab®** is packed with age-appropriate learning tools for fun, faith-building lessons. Toddlers & 2s explore big **Interactive StoryBoards**™ with enticing textures that toddlers love to touch—like sandpaper for earth, cotton for clouds, and blue cellophane for water. While they hear the Bible story, children also *touch* the Bible story. And they learn. **Bible Big Books**™ captivate Preschoolers and Pre-K & K while teaching them important Bible lessons. With **Jumbo Bible Puzzles**™ and involving **Learning Mats**™, your children will see, touch, and explore their Bible stories. Each quarter there's a brand new collection of supplies to keep your lessons fresh and involving.

Just order one **Learning Lab** and one **Teacher Guide** for each age level, add a few common classroom supplies, and presto—you have everything you need to inspire and build faith in your children. For more interactive fun, introduce your children to the age-appropriate puppet (Cuddles the Lamb, Whiskers the Mouse, or Pockets the Kangaroo) who will be your teaching assistant and their friend. No student books are required!

Hands-On Bible Curriculum is also available for elementary grades.

Order today from your local Christian bookstore, or write: Group Publishing, P.O. Box 485, Loveland, CO 80539.

BRING THE BIBLE TO LIFE FOR YOUR 1ST- THROUGH 6TH-GRADERS... WITH GROUP'S HANDS-ON BIBLE CURRICULUM™

Energize your kids with Authentic Learning!

In each lesson, students will participate in exciting and memorable learning experiences using fascinating gadgets and gizmos. Your elementary students will discover biblical truths and <u>remember</u> what they learn because they're <u>doing</u> instead of just listening.

You'll save time and money too!

Simply follow the quick and easy instructions in the **Teacher Guide**. You'll get tons of material for an energy-packed 35- to 60- minute lesson. Plus, you'll SAVE BIG over other curriculum programs that require you to buy expensive separate student books—all student handouts in Group's **Hands-On Bible Curriculum** are photocopiable!

In addition to the easy-to-use **Teacher Guide**, you'll get all the essential teaching materials you need in a ready-to-use **Learning Lab**®. No more running from store to store hunting for lesson materials—all the active-learning tools you need to teach 13 exciting Bible lessons to any size class are provided for you in the **Learning Lab**.

Challenging topics each quarter keep your kids coming back!

Group's **Hands-On Bible Curriculum** covers topics that matter to your kids and teaches them the Bible with integrity. Switching topics every month keeps your 1st- through 6th-graders enthused and coming back for more. The full two-year program will help your kids make God-pleasing decisions...recognize their God-given potential...and seek to grow as Christians.

Take the boredom out of Sunday school, children's church, and midweek meetings for your elementary students. Make your job easier and more rewarding with no-fail lessons that are ready in a flash. Order Group's **Hands-On Bible Curriculum** for your 1st- through 6th-graders today. (Also available for Toddlers & 2s, Preschool, and Pre-K and K!)

Order today from your local Christian bookstore, or write: Group Publishing, P.O. Box 485, Loveland, CO 80539.

Year-Round Fun for Your Children's Ministry

Bible Story Games for Preschoolers

Preschoolers learn by playing, and with these simple, age-appropriate games, children actually learn and *remember* Bible stories! You'll get 100 easy-to-do games that all tie in to Bible stories and use few or no supplies. These "everyone-wins" games help children feel good about church and themselves and give teachers a wide range of games to fit in with any Bible lesson.

ISBN 0-7644-2059-3 $15.99

Bible-Time Crafts Your Kids Will Love

From arks to zithers, each of these 47 crafts has a biblical and historical significance. That means you will use crafts again and again for dozens of Bible stories. Step-by-step directions make crafts easy, Bible background explains how items were used in Bible times, and a wrap-up activity for each craft helps kids use them at home.

ISBN 0-7644-2067-4 $14.99

Children's Church Specials

Here are 15 new, easy-to-lead worship sessions—each built around a specific characteristic of God! Children will learn to know and love God as they participate in upbeat praise, a memory-building activity, and worshipful prayer. As an added benefit, six of the worship services connect to holidays!

ISBN 0-7644-2063-1 $15.99

Strong & Simple Messages for Children's Ministry
Ruth Reazin

Make children's messages easy and memorable with these 53 flexible, quick-prep ways to teach Bible truths! Memorable object lessons drive home important Bible truths for kids—and make life easy for Sunday school teachers and children's workers! Perfect for high-impact children's sermons, lessons, and devotions.

ISBN 0-7644-2051-8 $12.99

Order today from your local Christian bookstore, or write: Group Publishing, P.O. Box 485, Loveland, CO 80539.